Puzzles from Pluto and beyond!

OUT OF THIS WORLD

Blast off to another dimension - don't forget your pencil case!

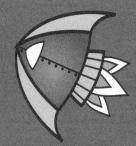

Visit our website at:
www.autumnchildrensbooks.co.uk

The Galaxy Gang

Meet the crew that will guide you on your space mission: there's perfect Pixel, the android who never leaves home without her pet, Pod. Then there's Ram, the robot who relishes a big puzzle challenge. He's joined by his cosmic companion, Bytes. Together, you can solve all the mysteries of outer space!

POD

PIXEL

Antenna dilemma

Which of your robotic friends has the longest antenna?

RAM

BYTES

The sky at night

Which two views through a telescope are exactly the same?

Gravity!

Pod's pal, Nano, is floating around without gravity.
Try drawing the same scene with gravity.

Rambling robot

Pixel's voice activator has developed a technical fault.
What is she trying to say?

WEL C OMETOO URP LAN ET.

_____

W EHOPEYO UENJ OYY OU
RSTA YHERE.

_____

Alien nation

Unravel the riddle to reveal which
planet this alien is from.

My first is in moon,
but not in soon.
My second is in star,
but not in stir.
My third is in rocket,
but not in pocket.
My fourth is in sun,
but not in bun.

prrrrrripp
SQUIBBLE!

I am from _____

Space race

Which space craft will make it to the home planet first?
Add the symbols together to find out.
The lowest number wins the race.

Space search

The search is on!
Check out this space challenge and find seven words
hidden in the grid – the pictures are clues!

```
S R O C K E T P S
P B E K Z D F C C
A D M O O N X L R
C J V D B G O X O
E Y I A M I A N B
S T A R Q F S F O
H N O B A E U B T
I B D S L O N K P
P L A N E T A X T
```

Pod's portrait

Draw a portrait of Pod in the grid, copying square by square.

Bytes' bug

Someone has corrupted Bytes' computer.
Help him crack the mysterious code left on his monitor.

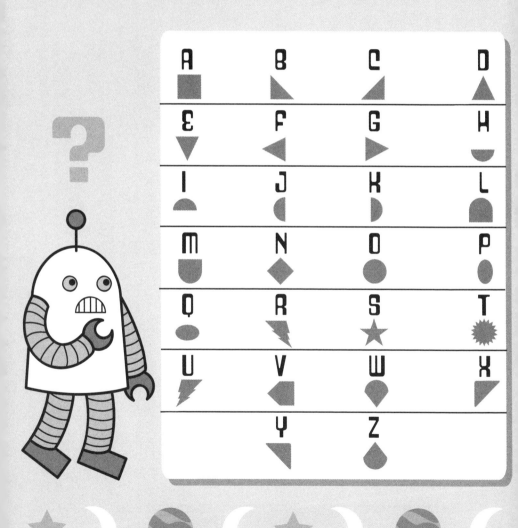

Space code

Now it's your turn to make up your very own alien code to share with your fellow astronauts. Draw some secret symbols under each letter of the alphabet.

A	B	C	D
E	F	G	H
I	J	K	L
M	N	O	P
Q	R	S	T
U	V	W	X
	Y	Z	

Now leave a cryptic coded message on this computer.

In a fix

Circle 10 differences between these two pictures.

Rhyming robots

Draw a line between the pairs
of rhyming robot twins.

PICK

MOLE

TREE

FLEA

COAT

KICK

BOAT

BOWL

We have lift off

Starting at number 23, count down and join the dots to complete the picture.

Designs on D.I.Y.

Ram has decided to try a bit of D.I.Y.
Help him decorate this rocket using great designs
and colours.

Trail blazing

Follow the vapour trails to get this alien home safely. You will spell out a message.

Cheesy moons

Unscramble the letters to reveal what cheese each moon is made of.

mead

zarellomza

dredach

A comet's tail

Complete the number patterns
in these comets' tails.

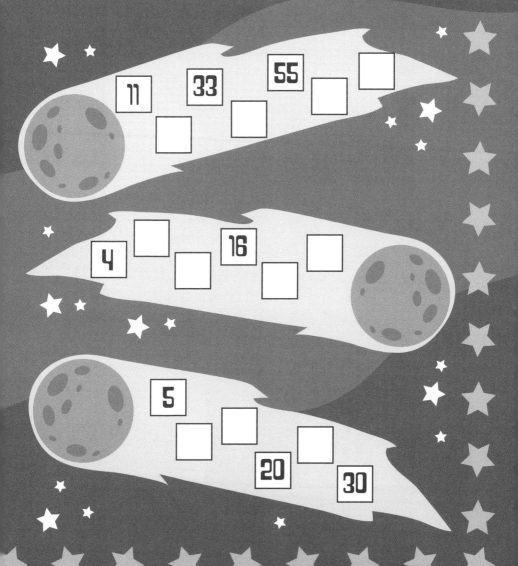

Robot fashion

Continue the patterns on these robots.

Annoyed android

This robot has stopped functioning!
Cross out the letters that appear twice to reveal
the activation code.

Silly space spotting

How many things can you spot that begin with the letter 's'?

Walking on the moon

How many astronauts have walked on this moon?
Write the number on the flag.

Lost in space!

Bytes has veered off course.
Guide him home by showing north east on the compass.

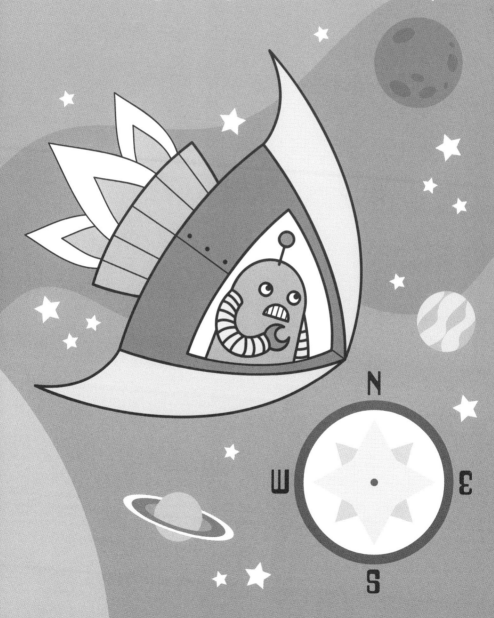

From a distance

Draw a view of Earth as you would see it from space,
then draw yourself in the rocket.

Use your head

These robots lost their heads in a crash!
Now they're all in a muddle. Can you join the bodies
to the right heads?

Meteor-right?

How many times can you make the word 'METEOR' using the letters below?

Alien alert

How many times does the word 'ALIEN' appear in this grid?

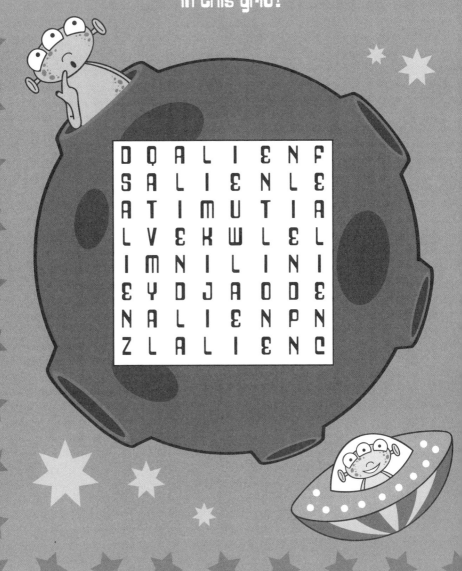

Draw a droid

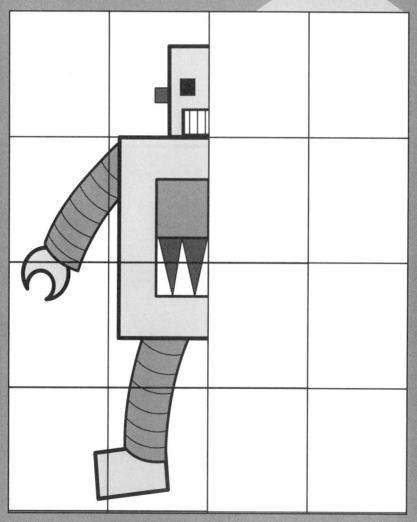

Martian madness

Things have gone a bit crazy in outer space!
Study this scene and circle anything that looks wrong.

Solar circles

How many circles can you
count in this scene?

Space oddity

Follow a star trail of odd numbers to guide Bytes back to the mother ship.

Undercover UFOs

How many hidden UFOs can you count in this picture?

Odd one out

Which Pod clone is the odd one out?

Old McRobot had a farm

Match the animals to their robot pals and make up silly names for the animal robots.

ANSWERS

Antenna dilemma
Bytes has the longest antenna.
The sky at night
Views a and e are the same.
Rambling robot
WELCOME TO OUR PLANET.
WE HOPE YOU ENJOY YOUR STAY HERE.
Alien nation
The alien is from Mars.
Space race
Space craft a wins the race.
Space search

Bytes' bug
WE COME IN PEACE.
TAKE US TO YOUR LEADER.
In a fix

Jupiter jigsaw
Piece b is missing.
Rhyming robots
PICK - KICK   MOLE - BOWL
TREE - FLEA   COAT - BOAT
Trail blazing
THERE IS LIFE ON MARS
Cheesy moons
Edam, mozzarella and Cheddar
A comet's tail
11, 22, 33, 44, 55, 66, 77
4, 8, 12, 16, 20, 24
5, 10, 15, 20, 25, 30

Annoyed android
ACTIVE
Silly space spotting
sun, stars, sandwiches, sunglasses, scarf,
strawberries, saucepan, sheep, shoes,
satellite, spider, spaceship, sausages, sock,
spoon, shorts, Saturn, stripes, sandcastle,
shells, spade, smile, spots, skirt.
Walking on the Moon
Six astronauts have walked there.
Lost in space

Use your head
1-e   2-c   3-d
4-f   5-b   6-a
Meteor-right?
6 times
Alien alert
7 times
Martian madness

Solar circles
There are 25 circles.
Cosmic match
1-6   2-12   3-10
4-8   5-9   7-11
Undercover UFOs
There are 14 hidden UFOs.
Odd one out
Clone 5 is the odd one out.